Sometimes doing less is the best gift a tired mom can give her family. Which is why I'm so grateful for Anna's stories. For how she opens her front door and invites us all in so that we can feel that we're OK with our own piles of laundry and imperfect traditions and Christmas cards we forgot to send. Because she reminds us over and over again in a hundred different examples that motherhood isn't about being perfect, it's about being present.
- Lisa-Jo Baker, *Author of Surprised by Motherhood: Everything I Never Expected About Being a Mom*

Simple daily devotions for YOU. It's so peaceful and encouraging!
- Amanda White, *Author of Truth in the Tinsel*

Anna gives heart-warming encouragement that's sure to put the joy back in your Christmas season. This busy mom is so grateful for Anna's honest advice and practical tips for reclaiming more moments of Christmas in my home this year!
- Sarah Cronin, *mom of 4 and owner of Simply Inspired Home Organizing*

This book is filled with real moments that we all experience. It is a calm moment in a hectic season.
- Jane Allen, *mom and grandmother*

Anna's words in this Advent devotional were exactly what I needed to hear during my first Advent as a mom (to a newborn, no less!)
- Sarah Knopf, *mom and crafter*

A Moment of Christmas

Daily Devotions for Time-strapped Moms

Anna Rendell

For Jared – I'm with you, for you, no matter what.
And for Sam, Josie & Clara – you're the best gifts
of my life. Christmas shines because of you.

You four have my whole heart.

Table of Contents

Foreword.................................…..…..9
Introduction..............................…..…..13
How to Use This Devotional...............…..…..17

Daily Devotions:
December 1 – December 25.............…..19-78

Prayers for Moms at Christmas:.............…..79
Prayer for the Parking Lot ....…....79
Prayer for Just One Perfect Place...........…..80
Prayer for Family Christmas Dinner ….....80
Prayer for Christmas Eve...............…........81
Prayer for Christmas Morning............…...…..81
Prayer for the New Year..................…....82

Acknowledgements ....…..…....83
About the author........................…..…....85

Foreword

The thing about becoming a mother for the first time is how much it changes your body. And how little you expect that. No one warned me about that part. I didn't have a mother to tell me that the pre-baby jeans I brought to the hospital I would absolutely *not* be wearing home.

That memory is what makes Mary so real for me. Because she and I have shared an earthy, bloody experience. She steps off the pages of history for me and into the hard, awkward reality of motherhood because we share a postpartum story.

It's also the reason I stopped singing *Silent Night* the first few years after becoming a mother. I couldn't stomach the words in the light of my new reality - experiencing birth and newborn nights from the inside out - nothing silent about it.

No -- birth in all its awkward, naked, aching reality was much more powerful than that.
It redefined me. And my idea of family and faith.

Because now when I look at my kids, when I look at my adopted siblings, I see in them how much God loves me. How He gave up heaven and Himself for me. How He spread His arms wide to misunderstanding and suffering, to gasps and agony and wanting it to be over and wanting to be released from this calling that cost Him so much.

This salvation, this redemption, this act of bearing children of the new covenant from His body through the mighty act of adoption and delivery on a cross.

We mothers, we get a front row seat at the wonder of Christmas because we've felt it in our weary bones and exhausted souls. How desperately we need peace from all our worries and fears.

And like you, I kneel beside my sleeping kids under Christmas twinkle lights, and I would do it all over again—the uncertainty, the heartache, the labor, the temper tantrums, and the sleep deprivation. Because it's all a gift. The gift of discovering that Jesus loves me this I know, for my children teach me so.

My daughter wants me to climb into bed with her on these cold evenings and she wraps her tiny arms around my head and neck and cradles me close, promising to always love me. We lie by the light of her Hello Kitty lights and I receive the love of a nearly six year old. Its weight is all the gold and myrrh and frankincense treasure in the world to me. And as I lie there receiving the unspeakable gift of unconditional love I feel my tired and weary soul rejoice.

Because Jesus came to love me and wrap His arms around me just like this - all of me. Not just the nice parts. The selfish parts too. The parts He's gently, tenderly rubbing away over years of parenting.

I don't need to perform for Him. I just need to receive.

I'm not always good at remembering that. Especially on the nights I'm snapping at my kids for how they're too loud or too messy or too dirty from all that raking leaves and how they're now traipsing it through my house. There are no silent nights here. But these nights on the princess bed or sofa or out back in the driveway under a basketball hoop or fighting over who gets to use the puppy Christmas wrapping paper are ours. They're our own story and it's a good one, even when it's not a perfect one.

I hope you know that yours is too.

Because there are no advent police.
There are no family traditions enforcers.
There are no report cards given on the kind of memories you're making.

Sometimes doing less is the best gift a tired mom can give her family. Which is why I'm so grateful for Anna's stories. For how she opens her front door and invites us all in so that we can feel that we're OK with our own piles of laundry and imperfect traditions and Christmas cards we forgot to send. Because she reminds us over and over again in a hundred different examples that motherhood isn't about being perfect, it's about being present.

It's OK. You're OK. You're more than OK.

You're knee deep in the sacred footsteps of Mary and her first loud, rough, desperate Christmas. You're there in the muck and the stink and the stable with her. Your kids still rowdy and unpredictable as hers on that first Christmas.

Grace, sisters, grace.

Because after all, it's Him that matters most. And He came to a tired mother with very little flourish, fancy, or perfect.

Love your tiny people, mamas. Crazy ordinary, without expectations love them and that will be more than enough.

From our an anything-but-silent house to yours,

Lisa-Jo Baker
Author of Surprised by Motherhood: Everything I Never Expected About Being a Mom

Introduction

Moms, we are the glue.

We are the ones who hold families together, who create traditions, who create warm holiday memories. We are the ones who remember the details, the permission slips, the dozen cookies for the preschool party, and the clean dresses for Christmas Eve church. We shop til we drop for our extended families, choosing just the right gifts for our {hard to please} relatives. We stamp envelopes, keep the address book updated, book family pictures and choose the right outfits to look coordinated (but not too matchy).

At least, we may feel like we're supposed to create and do all these things. So often, we – *and when I say "we," know that I mean "I"* – succumb to the lure of a Pinterest-worthy holiday, which only lands us in one of two places:

1) Wearing ourselves thin trying to pull off a perfect Christmas - homemade cookies decorated by our perfectly dressed and well-behaved children, an equal number of gifts for each child beautifully wrapped and under the tree before Christmas Eve, handmade gifts for the mailman and teachers and neighbors and grandmas, a burlap centerpiece on the dining table, stockings

hung by the chimney with care...

2) Or, feeling like a failure. No cinnamon rolls on Christmas morning? Fail. Finding a stack of un-mailed Christmas cards on December 26th? Fail. Having an argument with your husband while assembling toys in the wee hours of Christmas morning? Fail. Feeling like you didn't take in as much of the season as you could have? Fail.

Let's be honest. Either we make ourselves sick trying to pull off the perfect holiday, or we (most often) we land in the failure camp.

When we feel like a failure, guilt creeps in and occupies the space that joy should fill, which often brings on more guilt. It's a vicious cycle, and we pay the price by sacrificing our joy.

I can't even imagine Mary's face if someone were to describe this kind of guilt to her. I picture her trying to take it in: the idea that people share only their very best and decorated moments, and others feel badly when they can't re-create those scenes. Because in Mary's scene, there were smelly animals. There were name-callers. There was a donkey to transport her while she was in labor.

She RODE A DONKEY while she was IN LABOR. Let's let that sink in.

In her scene, she was a young girl pitted against the world, all while allowing her life to deliver glory to that world. Mary's burlap centerpiece lay in a manger – a feeding trough for animals – and her baby asleep in its hold.

Immanuel, God with us, delivered by a scared teenage couple in a rough, smelly stable full of animals. This was not a perfect and beautiful scene. Weddings weren't held in this barn; it had never seen a tealight or a mason jar.

But what it did see, what it did hold, was pure love.

Christmas gives us an opportunity to scrap expectations. The way Christ entered our world was so perfectly imperfect, full to bursting with love and joy, rough around the edges, and so very simple in its appearance. What if we embraced those standards – imperfection, love, joy, simplicity - amidst our to-do tasks and busy season?

As mothers, we can be champions for our children and professionals at neglecting ourselves – especially when it comes to the nourishment of our hearts. We will run ourselves ragged making sure our kids have amazing, memorable experiences. We don't sleep enough, we don't feed our bodies well, and we'll feel it fully, since everything is exaggerated during the Christmas season. Beginning with Thanksgiving and lasting through New Year's Day, we set ourselves up for disappointment and guilt as we continually put ourselves in last place.

Friends, this needs to change. Not only do we deserve to be cared for as we care for others, we have to show ourselves this care first.

Have you ever heard the airplane analogy? During the announcements given before a flight, flight attendants remind passengers to 'place an oxygen mask on yourself before trying to assist others." We need our own oxygen before we can be of any good to another. But as mothers, there is nothing we wouldn't do for our kids – including depriving ourselves of that which is life-giving.

That is why this book is for you. This book has been on my heart for a long time, and so have you. The woman being crushed under the weight of Pinterest-pressure. The woman so exhausted she hasn't read anything for herself in months or more. The woman desperate for connection with her own soul, with others, with Christ. The woman who craves a less-crazed feeling Christmas season, and longs for a season that is intentional and full of the joy that arises in knowing Christ is truly with us.

It's my prayer that, moment by moment, we will make room for the peace and full joy this season is meant to bring. I want my children to see me making room for Him in my inn, even amidst the to-do list. Whether at the beginning of the day before kids and life demand, or at the end of a long day before finally collapsing into bed - whenever you take a moment for yourself, I pray you allow the peace of the season to wash over you.

May the moments in this book be the guilt-free breaths of oxygen you've needed. May the stories and thoughts shared within the pages bring you peace instead of pressure, joy instead of guilt, convictions instead of expectations. And may you have yourself a merry little (moment of) Christmas.

Anna Rendell

How to Use this Devotional

Moms are busy. It's just a fact. So this devotional is designed to fit seamlessly into your especially tight December schedule. Toss it in your purse and read it while parked in the carpool pick-up line. Instead of your phone, reach for this book before rolling out of bed. Read at the breakfast table or when your kids are (supposed to be) napping. Whenever and wherever you decide to take your moment, each devotion is designed to be read in under ten minutes.

Each day includes several parts:
1. **Scripture** or inspirational quote
2. **Heart**: a short devotion just for you
3. **Pray**: written so you can simply pray, offering your heart to Him
4. **Ponder**: a question meant for you to carry in your mind throughout your day
5. **Hands**: something to do. A timesaving tip, recipe, tradition idea, etc.

Also included are six 'bonus moments' – short prayers for different situations & days.

Enjoy your moment of Christmas!

December 1

On those living in the land of deep darkness light has dawned.
Isaiah 9:2

Heart:
It's finally here. It's time to deck the halls, light the pine-scented candle, bake cookies, wrap gifts and celebrate His birth. The new page on the calendar is crisp and only just turned over, beckoning with possibilities. Before filling it to the brim with activities, pause. Take a breath. Think about the list of things you'd like to do this month – all the wonderful traditions and to-dos that are life-giving to you and to others. Does that list make you smile or make you weary?

Now look at that blank calendar again. On December 26th, what do you want to remember about your Christmas season? What sights and sounds do you want your heart and memories to be filled with? Move these things to the top of your list and schedule them first, because these are the things that bring you light.

Pray:
Father, thank you for this Advent season, for sending Your Son to be the Light in our darkness. Help me to fill this month ahead with the things that truly matter – to me, to You, to my family. Amen.

Ponder:
Think on the question posed above: on December 26th, what do you want to remember about your Christmas season?

Hands:
Start with your heart in the right place – start in prayer. Don't enter battle unarmed, the kitchen without ingredients, the holiday season without a heart open to Him. Because the only way to stay above water is to trust the One who walked on the waves.

December 2

Nothing is impossible with God.
Luke 1:37 (NIV)

Heart:
Oh, to our kids some things seem impossible.
Growing up, I recall:

- Christmas dinners that never seemed to end
- Visits to elderly family who smelled funny and served us 'weird' food like dates, pickled beets and lutefisk
- Wearing matching outfits with my siblings that included not-quite- dry turtlenecks

All I wanted to do was read my new books, sleep in, wear pajamas, eat the things I liked... it was all about me. Giving of myself was pretty far from my young and selfish mind. But what I learned from these family obligations (which, at the time, seemed impossible to bear) was that putting the joy of another before our own is a good thing. As moms, we know this to be true because we do it every day for our kids. But how often do we give them the chance to experience this kind of growth? Yeah, they may whine and protest, to which we can offer: "Nothing is impossible with God, kids."

While in context this verse speaks to events on a much grander scale, we can surely speak it over our kids' hearts when fulfilling family (and other 'boring') obligations. Perhaps they're not joyful in and of themselves, but these events serve as an antidote to selfishness and provide a lovely vessel for learning kindness and deep hospitality.

Pray:
Lord, may we not shy away from things we don't like at the expense of another's joy. Help me to provide uncomfortable experiences in kindness for my kids, and to fully participate in them myself. For nothing – even keeping a smile on my face – is impossible with You! Amen.

Ponder:
What opportunities for uncomfortable kindness can you provide your family and yourself this season?

Hands:
Buy a brand-new notebook (bonus points if it has a Christmas cover!) Make this your go-to place for storing to-do lists, shopping lists, ideas for gifts, a ledger of your purchases, etc. It will streamline your desk (and brain!) to have all those lists in one place rather than in mismatched sticky notes strewn around.

December 3

In the beginning the Word already existed. The Word was with God, and the Word was God. He existed in the beginning with God. God created everything through him, and nothing was created except through him. The Word gave life to everything that was created, and his life brought light to everyone. The light shines in the darkness, and the darkness can never extinguish it.
John 1:1-5

Heart:
It's happened more times than I care to admit. Inspired and excited, I place the Bible next to my bed and wait until bedtime to read a few verses. The first days go well, and I fall asleep with stories and characters and Scripture dancing through my heart. But then I get tired. The kids aren't sleeping well, I stayed up late working (or binging on Netflix), and I skip a night's reading so I can rest a little longer. I vow to renew my reading the next evening, but then... you know where this is going.

Though these verses in John are referring to Jesus, they apply to the written Word as well. If we move The Word to the beginning of our day, our hearts, our life, we'll be plugged into the Source from the start. And like the nightlights in our kids' rooms, it's only when we're plugged in that our light is able to shine. God promises that the Word gives life to all, that His Life gives Light that cannot be extinguished. This is deeply good news, friends.

So let's set the alarm for a few minutes before the

first child will wake. Let's release ourselves from guilt if we miss a day, and let's plug in. May we begin this Christmas season with the Word.

Pray:
Lord, I love Your Word. Thank you for the chance to read it, to take it in, to share it with my family. Help me to intentionally make space in my day to plug in to You. Amen.

Ponder:
What gets in the way of you being in the Word? What little changes can you make to combat that?

Hands:
Prep these caramel rolls at night, before bed. Then in the morning, get up a little earlier than usual. Make a cup of coffee, grab your Bible, and pop the rolls in the oven. You'll get a moment of peace, and your family will reap the benefits in more ways than one!

Christmas Morning Caramel Rolls

16 frozen bake-n-serve dinner rolls
1 - 3 ½ oz pkg. butterscotch cook-&-serve pudding mix
½ C. butter, melted
¾ C. brown sugar
1 C. chopped pecans, divided (*optional*)

The night before serving, sprinkle half the pecans in the bottom of a Bundt™ pan that's been sprayed with non-stick cooking spray. Arrange frozen dinner rolls on top of pecans; sprinkle with pudding mix.

Mix brown sugar and butter together; pour over rolls. Spread remaining pecans over top. Place pan uncovered in a cold oven and let stand overnight to rise.

In the morning, remove pan from the oven and preheat to 325 degrees. Return pan to oven; bake for 35 minutes.

Carefully turn pan upside-down onto a platter. Serves 4-8, with leftovers. Best with a cup of hot coffee.

December 4

The angel replied, "The Holy Spirit will come upon you, and the power of the Most High will overshadow you. So the baby to be born will be holy, and he will be called the Son of God."
Luke 1:35

Heart:
A couple years ago, my mother gave me an ornament that read, *'God rest ye merry gentlemen... the women are too busy!'*

As women, it seems that the joy of the holidays often falls on us to create. We are the glue that binds family, purchases the right gifts, gets them wrapped, coordinates activities, remembers church commitments, writes the Christmas cards, lights the candles, plans the meals... so when do we enjoy our silent nights? We don't want to take anything off our to-do lists, and, friends, that is okay. The items on our lists are there for a reason, and it's okay to keep them there. Often, they mean that we burn the midnight oil so that this will be a beautiful Christmas for those whom we love.

But what about our hearts?

When do we breathe? How do we enjoy this time of Advent? What must we loosen from our grasp so that we may instead grasp the tiny hands that make Christmas what it is – a birthday celebration of the highest importance?

Keep the things that matter on the list, moms, and

let go of the rest.

Pray:
Lord, above all I praise You. This is first, and the best way to prioritize – to think on what brings You praise and glory. The rest can fall to the wayside. I love You first, Lord – help me loosen, so that I may grasp. Amen.

Ponder:
What you could release from your list and/or calendar? What little thing(s) will keep until after the holidays?

Hands:
Spend some time with your calendar at the beginning of each Advent week. Try to plan as much as you can – meals, shopping trips and lists, kids' activities, church obligations, everything. If possible, share any family event plans with your spouse. Getting a solid game plan in your head will help keep you feeling organized the whole week!

December 5

And because Joseph was a descendant of King David, he had to go to Bethlehem in Judea, David's ancient home. He traveled there from the village of Nazareth in Galilee. He took with him Mary, his fiancée, who was now obviously pregnant. And while they were there, the time came for her baby to be born. She gave birth to her first child, a son. She wrapped him snugly in strips of cloth and laid him in a manger, because there was no lodging available for them.
Luke 2:4-7

Heart:
Let's talk about Mary, the mother of Jesus. Ladies, she rode a donkey while nearing labor.

She RODE A DONKEY while nearing LABOR.

She'd been teased and ostracized, chastened by an angel visit that shook her life and filled her soul. No doulas assisted, no nurses fussed. Only her husband was leaned on as he filled the roles of doctor, coach, and father. No onesies or tiny diapers were available, just strips of cloth from who knows where. No nursery to send Him to so she could rest, just the baleful eyes of donkeys and sheep.

She probably cried. I hope she let herself cry. And then I hope she let herself laugh till she cried again at the sheer bizarre and beautiful wonder of it all – the coming shepherds, the life her Son would live, the angel chorus making the night sky brilliant, a braying donkey the soundtrack, her new husband by her side, and a Babe. Her sweet baby boy, born to make her a mama and to make us whole.

And then she praised the One who orchestrated it all.

Pray:
Lord, we praise You. Right here, right now, I lift my heart in praise to You. This busy, messy, wonderful season is all about and for You. You deserve all of our wholehearted praise, and right here, right now, You have mine. Amen.

Ponder:
Right in the midst of your chaos, how are you praising the One who orchestrates your all?

Hands:
If you don't already have one, an Advent calendar is a great way to teach kids about waiting, and to help count down the days until Christmas together. While there are many varieties of Advent countdowns, our favorites include the classic cardboard boxes with chocolate behind each window, tiny sticker books, and books of short daily readings.

December 6

It is the sweet, simple things in life, which are the real ones after all.
- Laura Ingalls Wilder

Heart:
My kids think decorating the Christmas tree is amazing. They love it, maybe even more than their mama does (which is saying a lot). When my kids hang their ornaments, they are clumped at the bottom of the tree, hanging way down below the branches. They will show off their ornament branches and play with them until we take the tree down. (And let's not talk about when that happens. Because it's well past the twelve days of Christmas.)

Before we had kids, our Christmas tree looked very different – fragile, shimmering ornaments evenly distributed, packages carefully arranged underneath, and nothing made out of Popsicle sticks in sight. Since we now have small children, a few of the fragile ornaments have been lost. If the packages make it until Christmas Day unscathed, it's a miracle. Popsicle sticks, macaroni and glitter are now ever present on the green branches. It's nowhere near Pinterest-perfect – and it is absolutely wonderful.

Joy lives in the spirit of the giver, not in the presentation of the gift. I love what our tree now represents, in all of its mismatched, sweet, simple, low- branch clumped glory. It's our real life up there, and I couldn't love it more.

Pray:
Help me, Lord, to embrace Popsicle stick perfection. Nothing in my life belongs on Pinterest, and right now that's a good thing because my children are watching me live real. Help me to see Your glory reflected in my joyful mess. Amen.

Ponder:
What areas of your Christmas celebrations are less than perfect? If you're honest, why do they bother you (or why do you love them?)

Hands:
Set up a small artificial tree in your kids' bedroom! Let them decorate it as they wish, using their own special ornaments. My kids' tree includes colored lights and miniature ornaments that they love. Turn the tree on before bed so it serves as a nightlight.

December 7

How precious are your thoughts about me, O God.
They cannot be numbered! I can't even count them;
they outnumber the grains of sand!
Psalm 139:17-18

Heart:
We know what our kids love about Christmas. We rattle off their favorite traditions and events without a second thought:

"She loves baking with me, flour coating the counter and floor and ceiling. He loves to watch that certain holiday movie, wedged onto the couch and cuddled under blankets. They both stay awake in their beds on Christmas Eve, sleepily listening for sleigh bells. And if we don't have green, Christmas-tree shaped Jell-O for Christmas dinner, heaven help us."

We can name the silly, sweet, big and small things that matter most to our kiddos. But you, mom – what are YOUR favorite things about Advent and the Christmas season? What matters to your heart? Because that is important. If you need a few hours alone in front of the tree to regroup and refresh, ask your husband to take the kids out shopping and get yourself to that chair by the tree. If you love baking sugar-sparkled goodies, invite the kids into the kitchen to help. If decorating the house makes your heart pitter-pat, get a sitter for two hours and go to it kid-free.

Building in time for the things that make you say,

"NOW it feels like Christmas!" is important - vital - because you deserve to have the Christmas glow too.

Christmas is not just for kids. Jesus was born for you, too. Celebrate in the way that's right and meaningful to you!

Pray:
Lord, I am grateful that I matter to You. Thank you for the reminder that I am just as important as my kids are, and that it is okay to add some things that I love to our holiday traditions. Amen.

Ponder:
In this season, what are the traditions and activities that are most special to **your** heart? What can shuffle around in your schedule to make room for the things that feed your soul?

Hands:
As you deck the halls of your home, be intentional about the décor you set out. Do you really, truly love it? If not, place it in a separate bin. At the end of the season, donate whatever items are in that bin. Your home will be a little lighter and only decorated with the things you treasure, and who knows? Your lovely pieces may become the treasures of another family!

December 8

And she gave birth to her firstborn son and wrapped him in bands of cloth, and laid him in a manger, because there was no place for them in the inn.
Luke 2:7

Heart:
I am a perfectionist. I can't even say I'm a recovering perfectionist, because if I'm really honest I know I haven't given up those tendencies. I want things to be lovely and pretty close to perfect, and at times I've sacrificed the happiness of my family to obtain it. I've snapped at my husband, dressed my kids in cute, matching outfits instead of what they chose themselves, and stretched myself way too thin in the name of making perfect memories. I give up sleep and patience, and even kindness flies out the window in hopes of getting things perfect.

That first Christmas was less than perfect, yet it was glorious. It was the greatest mix of holy and human. There was straw, animal smell, and a star. There were hard hearts, new parents, and kings. At the start of the season, we have a choice to make. We can choose to chase perfection, or we can choose to chase holy.

When they are grown, what will make our kids nostalgic about their Christmases past? Let's make those the things that take center stage in our holiday celebrations. Our kids won't remember being late to church, the burned cookie debacle, or if the bathroom floor was clean. They will remember the warmth of their home, the traditions we start together, and most of all, they'll remember how we made them feel.

This year, let's drop perfect. Let's chase holy instead.

Pray:
Father, help me in this often stressful season to be patient, to remember that my family and friends will remember how I made them feel. Help me shepherd their feelings and focus on the things that matter. Grant me patience and joy so I may make my family feel special and cozy and loved by me. Grant me the openness to feel the same way by You. Amen.

Ponder:
What areas of perfection are you willing to drop? What do you think you'll actually gain if things are less than perfect?

Hands:
Let your kids help for real. Give them jobs that matter. Let them sign the Christmas cards, cut out the cookie dough, set the table, hang the breakable ornaments on the tree... Will it take longer? Maybe. Will it be worth it? Absolutely. They will feel your trust and give you the gift of their imperfection and love.

December 9

Long ago the LORD said to Israel: "I have loved you, my people, with an everlasting love. With unfailing love I have drawn you to myself."
Jeremiah 31:3

Heart:
Has it been one of **those** days? Are you feeling a little defeated, defensive, alone? Have you said something you regret? Are the kids running amuck? And is it only 9:00 am?

Take a breath. You need to know that you – yes, you – are doing a fantastic job. There is no other time of year that may make us feel more inadequate, pressed for time, impatient and comparison-filled than Christmas. Isn't that sad? I'm pretty sure that's not what He had in mind when a lowly stable was filled with His glory, housed in a baby.

So today, however much is left of it, know deep down that you are enough because He is enough in you. Your Christmas is enough – for your kids and your family – because of the love you have poured into it. And at the end of the day, if the only things you've accomplished are having kept the kids out of the presents, fed them and yourself, and given a bunch of hugs, then, mama -- you did it, it was enough, and you are loved unfailingly.

Pray:
Lord, fill me with Your patience, love and joy today, because I do not have these things on my own. Stay with me as I try to parent well and cram more into

this day than is possible, and help me to do it with grace. Give me the peace that passes understanding, and when my head hits the pillow tonight, assure me that today I have been enough because You are. Amen.

Ponder:
When you're having one of **those** days, what small things can you do to get it back on track?

Hands:
Do you have a collection of Christmas CD's? Keep them all in one case! That way, when you're heading out of the house, you can just grab the case and be on your way with some Christmas cheer. If you don't have CD's anymore, create a Christmas-only playlist on Spotify or your phone. Pull it up and sing along! (Find a few ideas to get you started here: http://bit.ly/amocplaylist)

December 10

"I think there must be something wrong with me, Linus. Christmas is coming, but I'm not happy. I don't feel the way I'm supposed to feel."
- Charlie Brown, A Charlie Brown Christmas

Heart:
For some, Christmas can be a time of anguish and pain. Missing family members who are no longer in our lives, bearing the marks of infertility, financial problems, and more can impede the supposed joy of the season.

Remember when poor Charlie Brown confesses this to his friend, Linus? We have high expectations of our feelings because "it's Christmas!" We are supposed to be rejoicing and feeling all the warm fuzzies! We are supposed to set the tone for joy! But sometimes we just aren't able to do this. And you need to know that there is no guilt in feeling your very real, very valid, emotions.

God welcomes our honesty. He wants us to bring Him the nitty-gritty of our feelings, the raw emotions we often suppress because He sees you. He sees the pain and fears you've been hanging on to, and He beckons welcome. There is no 'supposed to.' There is only Him, and He invites your all.

Pray:
God, You know my struggle. You know my pain. I want to be happy, but Lord... I'm not sure how I'm supposed to feel. So I bring it all to You. I place this pain, this unknown and confusion, in Your hands,

and I ask for Your healing to be bigger than my despair. I love You, and I trust You with this. Amen.

Ponder:
What pain are you harboring this year? Are you able to bring it to the Lord – why or why not?

Hands:
Scent can be a path of comfort to our heart. It can set the tone for our home, creating a space of comfort and joy. And it can just plain old make it feel like Christmas!

Make a batch of this super simple Stovetop Potpourri to bring holiday scent into your home (without inhaling any icky toxins or chemicals.) Better yet, double the recipe and gift it to a friend! She'll be touched by your thoughtfulness.

Stovetop Holiday Potpourri

One orange, quartered (leave whole if gifting)
1/2 C. fresh cranberries
1 Tbs. whole cloves
3 cinnamon sticks
1 tsp. grated nutmeg
1 bay leaf

Place all ingredients in a small saucepan filled with water. Simmer on low heat, refilling water as needed.

If preparing to give as a gift, place all ingredients in a paper bag. Tuck a copy of these instructions inside:

Quarter the orange. Place all ingredients in a small saucepan filled with water. Simmer on lowest setting, refilling water as needed. Breathe deeply, and have yourself a moment of peace.

December 11

Silent night, holy night All is calm, all is bright... *

Heart:
Our schedules are already full, and the Christmas season adds to the chaos. Parties to attend, gatherings to host, volunteering, special services at church, traditions to uphold, dinners to plan... the list goes on. And it's a good list!

But where on your own list do you fall? Are you even on it? If so, I bet you're toward the bottom, and we all know what happens to the bottom of our lists. They're the first to get crossed off, undone.

If you're not high up on your own list, the season is going to overtake you like a strong current. Has it already? Are you going under? Right now, stop. Just take one moment to breathe. Remember the airplane analogy - put on your oxygen mask before assisting others? This is the time. Get that oxygen mask on so you will be able to do all that you want to do to help your family experience the joy of this season!

Mom, get thee a silent night and take a moment to steep in wonder.

Pray:
Holy Father, this season... it is miraculous indeed, and so is Your love. We are celebrating this wondrous thing that happened thousands of years ago, yet Your love for me is as strong now as it was then. May I slow down enough, even just for a

moment, to embrace that love and peace. Amen.

Ponder:
What can you intentionally work into your busy schedule to make sure you're refreshing yourself? A date night, a quiet evening by the fire, a calming CD in the car – what works best to calm and refresh your soul?

Hands:
Actively plan for a quiet night after the kids are in bed – even though it's late and there are projects to check off. You deserve to give yourself a gift of time. So mark your calendar and keep this appointment!

Make a cup of hot cocoa or tea. Light the room only by the Christmas tree lights and maybe a favorite scented candle, and curl up under a quilt. Use these few quiet moments to breathe, slow and deep, and reflect on what this season of miracles means to you.

*Lyric from *Silent Night*. Hymn in public domain.

44

December 12

The Lord himself will give you the sign. Look! The virgin will conceive a child! She will give birth to a son and will call him Immanuel (which means "God is with us.")
Isaiah 7:14

Heart:
The Christmas story seems a little impossible, doesn't it? From prophecies long foretold coming true, a virgin conception, a barnyard birth... the whole thing is something only a big, loving God could've orchestrated and carried out. He asked people to do incredibly difficult things, to witness miracles, to believe the actual impossible, and then He delivered.

Elizabeth and Zechariah, in their old age, were asked to believe. Mary, an unwed teenager, was asked to believe. The Magi, miles and years away from meeting the child Savior, were asked to believe. Joseph, betrothed to a woman carrying someone else's child, was asked to believe.

Not only did God ask them all to believe, but He asked them to believe in good things. Sometimes those are the hardest things to trust because we fear what may happen if the other shoe drops. God asked the people in the Christmas story to believe in His goodness, to buy into the good and make their fear smaller than their belief.

And today, God is asking us to believe the same.

No matter what we're facing this season, this day - this moment! – We can believe and trust that He is good, and that He is *doing* good in our life.

Pray:
God, help my unbelief. Where You are working for good in my life, help me embrace it more than I embrace the fear of the flip side. Help me trust in the impossible good that comes from You. Amen.

Ponder:
What impossibility are you facing? What impossible good is He asking you to believe?

Hands:
Dinner feeling impossible? Spend a day or two deep in your kitchen prepping freezer meals for busy days during December! Just a few hours will turn out several meals. Your freezer will be stocked, your budget will be on track (both financial and calorie budgets satisfied), and your family will thank you because instead of PBJ's or scrambled eggs their bellies will be full with delicious, hot food. And you won't be stressed about what to make. Win win.

December 13

For a child is born to us, a son is given to us. The government will rest on his shoulders. And he will be called: Wonderful Counselor, Mighty God, Everlasting Father, Prince of Peace.
Isaiah 9:6

Heart:
Jesus, the tiny babe who came to save the world, was once a child with a mother. His mother (much like you) surely did her very best to be gentle and kind and creative with her babies. She quite possibly tried to be all things, just like we do. Except we are not made to be all things – both in big and small ways. As moms, we are not all Pin-worthy decorators, top chefs, and amazing bakers. We do not all love to make crafts with our kids. We do not all excel at shopping for the perfect gift, serving on the church committee, and entertaining family & friends over a meal. We may be gifted in one or more of these areas, but no one is fabulous at them all.

We are not all things, especially at Christmas. When I try to be all things in one day – working mom, stay-at-home mom, great cook, creative kid-entertainer, art director, shopper extraordinaire – I am a wreck by noon. We cannot be all things to all people. We can't even be all things to our kids, our spouses, or to ourselves.

The good news? There is One who can be all things! He is a Wonderful Counselor, Mighty God, Everlasting Father, Prince of Peace. Only Jesus, the one who came to make a mother and save the world, is all things. Only Him. Not us. This is truly good news.

Pray:
Jesus, thank You. Thank You for being so, so much more than me. Thank You for filling all these roles and more. Help me lay at your feet the roles I don't need to fill. Amen.

Ponder:
What roles do you try to force yourself to take on when you don't feel equipped and/or don't enjoy them? How can you let these go?

Hands:
This foolproof fudge recipe is just that – super easy and super delicious. Make a batch to gift a friend, teacher or your own family.

Foolproof Microwave Fudge

3 cups high quality semisweet chocolate chips
1 – 14oz. can sweetened condensed milk
1 tsp. vanilla
Toppings (optional): crushed candy canes, mini red and green candies, sprinkles, etc.

Line an 8x8 pan with wax paper. Use too much paper so it hangs over both sides of the pan. Spray with non-stick vegetable spray.

In a large microwave-safe bowl, combine chocolate chips and sweetened condensed milk. Microwave on high for 2 minutes, then slowly stir in vanilla until the mixture is smooth.

Pour mixture into prepared pan. If you want to add toppings, press them gently in the top of the fudge now.

Let cool on the countertop until mostly firm, then lift out wax paper, and cut into squares.

December 14

And the one sitting on the throne said, "Look, I am making everything new!"
Revelation 21:5

Heart:
There are years when the celebrations seem wan and pale, even trite. Years when, for whatever reason, you find yourself going through the motions, unable to really take it all in. Years when the things that used to make the celebrating sweet now seem overdone and saccharin. What's a mom to do when traditions get stale?

Take a breather. Sit down and center your heart. Recall a stable scene long ago, with a young family and angel choruses, sheep and shepherds, magi en route, and a new mama smitten with her Son. There were no traditions for them yet, as the Reason to celebrate had just arrived. They didn't hop on Facebook or Twitter to see what all the other families were doing to celebrate. No, they simply soaked up their own new family, quietly reveling in what the Lord was up to.

There is so much we can glean from that first Christmas. When you need a breath of fresh Christmas air, when all the usual ways you celebrate and recognize the holiday seem old and uninspired, when it seems things have been said many times, many ways... take a moment and recall the One who makes all things new.

Pray:
God, I need a little breath of fresh air today. Things are feeling kind of flat, a little forced, and I want them to be renewed and full. Breathe Your spirit into my heart today, Lord, and into the heart of our celebrations. Amen.

Ponder:
What parts of your traditions feel like they've been done many times, many ways? What would it take to make them feel new again?

Hands:
Have a cookie swap with friends! It's easier than you may think. Bake or buy 2-dozen cookies (or bars, or dipped pretzels, or whatever deliciousness you like.) Invite friends to bring their own treats to contribute and gather around your table. Set all the goodies out. Walk around the table taking 2-3 of each cookie until they are evenly distributed to all attendees. Everyone goes home with about 2-dozen different cookies – not too many, not too few, and all new to you! Easy as that.

December 15

An angel of the Lord appeared to them, and the glory of the Lord shone around them, and they were terrified. But the angel said to them, "Do not be afraid. I bring you good news that will cause great joy for all the people. Today in the town of David a Savior has been born to you; he is the Messiah, the Lord. This will be a sign to you: You will find a baby wrapped in cloths and lying in a manger." Suddenly a great company of the heavenly host appeared with the angel, praising God and saying, "Glory to God in the highest heaven, and on earth peace to those on whom his favor rests."
Luke 2:9-14 (NIV)

Heart:
The shepherds. Mary. Joseph. The wise men, and even the innkeeper on that holy night. Mingled into the wondrous beauty of the Christmas story, there are those who experienced fear of it. Angels had to reassure Mary and Joseph in their fear. The Magi chose the wise but fearful route to flee from Herod's orders. The innkeeper was asked for a room and had to turn away a woman in labor – and if that didn't strike fear into his heart, I don't what would!

And these precious shepherds. Can you imagine? Being in the quiet countryside, nearing sleep, their sheep tucked in for the night. The campfires burning embers, stoked just enough to keep warm. The dishes were done, the work completed for the day, and all was still. Then suddenly, throngs of angels, singing and shining! Not just glowing like the star at the top of your tree – no, it was the unfiltered glory of the Lord that shone in Technicolor! Gone was the stillness, and their first reaction was fear. Not that I blame them, or anyone else who was afraid of God and His messengers, because sometimes the thing God asks us to do or the method He uses to ask us is terrifying.

The thing is, a fear of Him is good – healthy, even. He is GOD, after all! Yet in all these first Christmas instances, despite their fear, the people who heard Him obeyed and were sovereignly blessed by the outcome.

God is good, even when we are afraid of Him or the good that He is doing in our lives.

Pray:
Lord, sometimes your glory scares us. Sometimes seeing Your glory in ourselves and in others scares us. But we know You are good, and we know you're doing good in us. May our hearts be beautifully fearful of You. Amen.

Ponder:
What is something you feel God is asking of you that is frightening, but good?

Hands:
Count down the last few days until Christmas with an old-school paper chain. Easy and fun for kids to put together, you could even add an activity, prayer or hope on each daily link. Remove a link before bed each night until Christmas Day!

December 16

Therefore I tell you, do not worry about your life, what you will eat or what you will drink, or about your body, what you will wear. Isn't life more than food, and your body more than clothing?
Matthew 6:25

Heart:
Sometimes when I'm really happy and enjoying life, I worry that the other shoe is going to drop. If there's not chaos somewhere in my days, I almost feel guilty and I definitely feel worried. What kind of living is that?

There is no guilt in enjoying your days, in loving your life, in celebrating the little moments that may actually be the big ones.

Today, let your heart be light. Soak up this day of Advent, this day with your family, this day of big and little things, of delights and disappointments, of highs and lows. Make a very intentional decision to let your heart be light, and to have a merry little Christmas indeed.

Pray:
Father, You tell us to not worry about anything – big or small. I want to enjoy this season in all its complex simplicity, and I want to have a light heart that's full of joy. Help me let go of the heaviness I'm carrying, and – even just for today – live light and merry. Amen.

Ponder:
Why is it almost easier to gravitate to a heavy heart than a light one? What do you need to let go of in order to embrace a light heart?

Hands:
Clean out your closets! Gather the things that are in great shape but that you and your family don't absolutely love, and donate them. Allow yourself only a small pile (read: 5 pieces) of clothing that are in the 'someday I may wear this again' category. Begin the New Year lightened, simplified, and blessing others.

December 17

*Glory to God in highest heaven, and peace on earth
to those with whom God is pleased.*
Luke 2:14

Heart:
I struggle with "not fair-itis." You know – the
feeling that creeps in when someone else gets an
opportunity I'd like to have or feel I deserve? Or
when their family appears more put together than
the three-ring circus I have at home, or when she
fits into their pre-baby jeans at three days
postpartum and I don't three years after giving
birth... The last thing I feel in these situations is
peace.

All the major players of the Christmas story could
absolutely have had "not fair- itis." Joseph was
engaged to a girl who was pregnant, and not with
his child. Not fair! Mary was pregnant beyond her
control, and must travel while nearing and during
labor. Not fair!

Yet they obeyed, and God was pleased with them.
Scripture doesn't share many of their emotions with
us – with the exception of Mary's joy and song. She
rejoices in the unfair love of the Lord.

You read that right. It's absolutely unfair how
deeply He loves us, that He is pleased with us, and
that we are constantly in His favor no matter our
circumstances. When you start slipping into a fit of
unfair-itis, remember how He loves us in spite of,
because of, and no matter what – just like He did

Mary.

Pray:
Lord, Your love is so big – big enough to cover my petty thoughts of fairness. Help me to obey and love like Mary, despite the unfair feelings of the situation. Everything about You and Your grace is unfair in the very best way. Amen.

Ponder:
What things trigger feelings of unfairness in your heart? How can you head them off, choosing a peaceful heart instead?

Hands:
Make an entire night out of going to pick out the perfect Christmas tree - even if your tree lot is in the grocery store parking lot! Bring mugs of hot cocoa or cider, crank up the Christmas tunes, and take your time choosing just the right tree. Even if the kids melt down, have to go potty in the middle of the woods, and spill their cocoa, you'll make plenty of sweet real-life memories!

December 18

This is how Jesus the Messiah was born. His mother, Mary, was engaged to be married to Joseph. But before the marriage took place, while she was still a virgin, she became pregnant through the power of the Holy Spirit. Joseph, her fiancé, was a good man and did not want to disgrace her publicly, so he decided to break the engagement quietly. As he considered this, an angel of the Lord appeared to him in a dream. "Joseph, son of David," the angel said, "do not be afraid to take Mary as your wife. For the child within her was conceived by the Holy Spirit. And she will have a son, and you are to name him Jesus, for he will save his people from their sins." All of this occurred to fulfill the Lord's message through his prophet: "Look! The virgin will conceive a child! She will give birth to a son, and they will call him Immanuel, which means 'God is with us.'" When Joseph woke up, he did as the angel of the Lord commanded and took Mary as his wife.
Matthew 1:18-24

Heart:
This story is one of holy obedience. If just one player in the grand story decided to go their own way, to reply "No" to the call, to ignore the sound of that still, small voice, God would surely have found a way, but it wouldn't be the story we know and cherish. He always finds a way, but if our hearts are soft to His first idea, things seem to go more smoothly. It's like we tell our kids – to please listen the first time we ask. God used the first-time obedience of Mary and Joseph, the shepherds and

even the innkeeper to carry out His holy plan.

He still uses our obedience today. What incredible things could He accomplish in our lives, hearts and families if we gave Him a yes the first time He called?

Pray:
Lord, I want to hear You clearly and not delay in my yes. Your plans for our life are glorious, and I want to be used to point to Your glory. So I ask for courage to say yes to You in even the strangest things You ask of me. I ask for grace when I would rather run, and strength to teach my children the same. Amen.

Ponder:
What would look different about our lives if we practiced first-time obedience to the Lord's leading?

Hands:
I've made this recipe for Eggnog Quick Bread every Christmas for the past ten years. It makes a bread that's not overly sweet, not too "noggy," and the top of the loaf gets caramelized and delicious. It makes a great breakfast, a lovely gift for a friend, and freezes beautifully.

Eggnog Quick Bread

2 eggs
1 C. sugar
1 C. eggnog
½ C. butter, melted
1 tsp. vanilla
2 ¼ C. all-purpose flour
2 tsp. baking powder
¼ tsp. nutmeg

Preheat oven to 350 degrees.

Beat eggs in a large bowl, and then add sugar, eggnog, butter and vanilla to bowl. Blend well. Set aside.

In separate bowl, combine flour, baking powder and nutmeg. Add flour mixture to eggnog mixture and stir until just combined.

Pour into a greased 9×5 loaf pan and bake at 350 degrees for about 70 minutes (or until center tests done).

Let cool for 10 minutes, then remove from pan and let cool completely. Slice and enjoy!

December 19

"Look! I am sending my messenger, and he will prepare the way before me. Then the Lord you are seeking will suddenly come to his Temple. The messenger of the covenant, whom you look for so eagerly, is surely coming," says the LORD of Heaven's Armies. Malachi 3:1

Heart:
He came. Jesus came to pave the way for His Father, to show us God with skin on.

And so we celebrate – with twinkly lights, choirs singing, treats a-plenty, thoughtful gifts, family gatherings, and trees adorned. We anticipate the remembrance of His coming with seeking and eager joy.

Today, think on the preparing. What type of preparation does your home need in order for you to be joyful? We're not talking a deep-clean kind of preparing, but if dusting would settle your heart, go for it. In what ways does your heart need preparation for Christmas? More quiet time, diving into the to-do list, making snow angels with your 5-year-old? What things need to be done in the few days left before Christmas to prepare the way for Him to enter your heart?

Think on your answers, make space for them in your schedule, and let the rest fall. Let's be intentional about keeping the main things in the spotlighted center stage of our lives, and keep our hands open to release the rest.

Pray:
*Lord, help me to keep my main things the main
things. You, my family, then the extras. May I keep
the path to my heart cleared – paved – for You to
easily enter in. Amen.*

Ponder:
Are there unfinished projects on your list that are
bothering you? Can you finish them, or would you
be okay to let them fall off the list?

Hands:
Simple: only buy wrapping paper you really like, be
it bright & shiny or brown kraft paper. 'Tis the
season of joy, friends, and that includes the littlest
things. Why spend HOURS wrapping and staring at
patterns that don't bring joy to our hearts? I know.
It's wrapping paper. Not a big deal. Kind of a small
one, actually. But if we set the precedent of
bringing only items that we treasure into our home,
and if we start with the littlest of things, we'll start
to build muscle memory. The idea will begin to
shift our hearts and lead our actions. So start with
wrapping paper, and go from there.

December 20

John the Baptist, who was in prison, heard about all the things the Messiah was doing. So he sent his disciples to ask Jesus, "Are you the Messiah we've been expecting, or should we keep looking for someone else?"
Matthew 11:2-3

Heart:
While he was in prison, John had his disciples ask Jesus the hard questions that he could not hold back, and we are welcomed to do the same.

Because God doesn't want our "fine." God wants our "real."

Sometimes Christmas is difficult, even amidst the wonderful, and we may not even know why. Our fears and sadness may rise to the surface and nothing we do can stop the flood of feelings. Amidst the bustle, the baking, the wrapping and the good cheer, I pray you let yourself feel whatever rises to the top of your heart this Christmas. Sadness, joy, guilt, exhaustion, nostalgia, a deep ache for those gone and missing from our table -- whatever the emotion, Christ came for its release.

His birth is our beginning too, and that precious Babe in the manger is big enough to lean into weeping. As the carol sings, '*The hopes and fears of all the years are met in Thee tonight.*'* Every single one, met in Him.

May peace be yours, during this - the most wonderful and difficult time of the year.

Pray:
Lord, I have a lot of emotions this Christmas. In my feeling of them all, You are gracious and I am grateful. Help me to lean into You when I am overwhelmed, be it with sadness or joy -- in this season and all my seasons. Amen.

Ponder:
Spend some time giving space to hard feelings this season: memories, grief, whatever the struggle is. Journal, talk it through with a friend, and pray deeply. Let yourself feel those emotions without adding guilt on top.

Hands:
Load up the minivan and go for an evening drive! Whether by yourself or with the whole family, bring a thermos of hot tea or cocoa, crank the Christmas tunes, and set out to find local light displays.

*Lyric from *O Little Town of Bethlehem*. Hymn in public domain.

December 21

Wait patiently for the Lord. Be brave and
courageous. Yes, wait patiently for the Lord.
Psalm 27:14

Heart:
A couple of years ago we stepped back after
unloading the bins of Christmas decorations, and
realized it looked like Christmas had "thrown up" in
our house. We realized there was no space in
between one decorated area and another – every
surface was covered! We needed some open space
for our beautiful decorations to be properly
highlighted and enjoyed.

In the same way, it's the empty space between the
celebrations, the ornaments, and the special times
that make them able to shine. That emptiness – the
visually quiet space – is called peace, and it's a big
part of what Christmas is about.

Peace found it's way to the first Christmas. The
night began with a stressful and chaotic attempt to
find a place to have the baby. Afterward, the
contents of heaven were displayed in the most
intense manner ever shown to earth, as angels filled
the sky and sang in full belting voices. And in
between, The Baby was born. The birth itself was
probably not peaceful, but in some of the moments
following, there was quiet. There was peace.

Christ came in peace. He is for peace – in our hearts
and in our lives, in both big and small ways.

Pray:
Lord, fill this heart, this home, this family, with peace -- the kind that only comes from You and can be felt deeply, quietly, in the in-between. Help us to provide You with space this season, and to notice Your presence in it. Amen.

Ponder:
What's waiting for you this Christmas in the empty spaces, in the 'in between' of your busy-ness? Where are you finding peace?

Hands:
Time for another quiet evening. Put away all the noise for an evening. Light a candle, turn on the Christmas tree lights, make a cup of hot chocolate and just soak in the peace (even if it's only five minutes before you're interrupted!) Not only is it good for your soul to rest, it's good to model this kind of peaceful and restful behavior to our families.

December 22

No one lights a lamp and then covers it with a bowl or hides it under a bed. A lamp is placed on a stand, where its light can be seen by all who enter the house. For all that is secret will eventually be brought into the open, and everything that is concealed will be brought to light and made known to all.
Luke 8:16-17

Heart:
Christmas is a perfect time to let our lights shine in public. There are countless volunteer opportunities, donation centers, bells to ring, general goodwill and merriment to spread... But what about the chances we have to shine in our own homes? To choose goodwill over frustration, to volunteer instead of demand, to ring of joy rather than discord?

Do you ever feel like it's easier to be a better person to those outside our homes than to the ones in it? Simple honesty – I struggle with this. Sometimes it's exhausting to shine, and home is a place to rest. But simply because we are in our real, messy, everyday lives doesn't mean that we get to conceal the light that He has placed in us. It means we're called to shine it that much brighter, and it's also that much harder to do!

Home is where you can be your worst self, and still be loved and accepted. So to shine at home as you do in public can go against a regular pattern of coming home and falling apart, where it's safe to do so. While it will definitely be a challenge to shine within our own walls, it's one that comes with promise of growth for our whole families. It is worth every struggle that comes as a result of choosing to let our light shine brightest right in our own homes.

Pray:
Lord, help the woman I am at home match or even exceed the woman I am in public. Give me strength when it would be so much easier to hide my shine under the bed with the dust bunnies. Help me choose to place the lamp on a stand in my own home this season. Amen.

Ponder:
When is it most difficult for you to shine your light at home? How can you intentionally struggle through that in order to shine brightly?

Hands:
I discovered this recipe several years ago just days before my first child was born. Five years later, he's the first one in line to grab a handful. We've got our tweaks down and this is still one of our family's favorites holiday season treats!

Peppermint Popcorn Crunch

2 bags microwave popcorn*
1 bag vanilla candy melts
¼ tsp. peppermint extract**
1 Tbs. vegetable oil
1-2 bag(s) mint chocolate candies
Christmas sprinkles

Pop the popcorn as directed.

Pour onto a rimmed cookie sheet. Remove as many un-popped kernels as you can, then pour popcorn into large bowl.

In separate glass bowl, melt the candy melts for 1 minute, then for 30-second intervals, stirring between each time until melted. Stir in vegetable oil and peppermint extract.

Pour mixture over the popcorn and mix together. It's messy but works best to dig in with your hands! Add the mint chocolate candies and Christmas sprinkles. Toss everything together (again, dig in with your hands!)

If you're feeling generous, put a scoop of popcorn in a little bag, tie with a ribbon and bring to a friend. But if you eat the whole batch yourself, I won't judge.

Notes:
*Substitute a large batch of stovetop or air-popped popcorn for the microwaved bags. Add melted butter and a few generous pinches of kosher salt to the plain popcorn.

**Peppermint oil is a good alternative if you don't have extract. If you use peppermint oil, only add 2 drops.

December 23

Look at my Servant, whom I have chosen. He is my
Beloved, who pleases me. I will put my Spirit upon
him, and he will proclaim justice to the nations. And
his name will be the hope of all the world.
Matthew 12:18, 21

Heart:
Injustice seems bigger at Christmas. The poor seem
powerless and many, the needs of the world seem
greater, and our resources seem even smaller than
usual. Is it because our hearts enlarge with hope
during these holy days? Or are the injustices and
our hearts always this big, but our vision slightly
cloudy the rest of the year? Either way, we know
that while we can't champion for all the causes, we
can make a difference to a few.

What makes your heart beat fast for people? Is it
poverty, trafficking & slavery, or water unclean to
drink? Is it homelessness, abused & abandoned
animals, or the environment? Jesus came to bring
justice, and He uses our hands to help. Choose the
causes that resonate with your – and your family's –
heart. Support those organizations this holiday
season, and trust that while the needs are many and
the resources few, Jesus has not forgotten that His
name is hope.

Pray:
Lord, sometimes I feel small. In light of so many
struggles, my offering seems meager. Will You make
it bless? Will You take it and go all loaves and
fishes on it, multiplying its worth? Most

importantly, put in my heart a passion for the needs of Your people. Amen.

Ponder:
What is one cause you can give to this year, be it from your time, talents or treasures?

Hands:
In addition to the whole giving back/doing good aspect, the convenience of donating online can't be beat. Most websites even provide a customizable printable for your recipient. Easy and impactful? Yes please! Here are a few of my favorite organizations to donate to:

- Samaritans Purse (Operation Christmas Child) - http://www.samaritanspurse.org/
- World Vision - http://donate.worldvision.org/ways-to-give/gift-catalog
- International Justice Mission - http://ijm.org/
- Heifer International - http://www.heifer.org/

December 24:
Christmas Eve

Anyone who becomes as humble as this little child is the greatest in the Kingdom of Heaven. Matthew 18:4

Heart:
Is there any more wonder-filled day for kids than Christmas Eve? They're out of school (magical in and of itself), knowing two days of traditions are about to unfold, while presents beckon and stockings await filling... And you know they'll lie awake long into the night listening for the peal of silvery sleigh bells.

Children are awe-filled at Christmas. Beyond any tired, tantrum, and cranky they can churn out, there is wonder. The simple sights and smells of the season charm their hearts, and their eyes are open to how extraordinary our ordinary days are.

Do you feel you've lost the "childlike" from your faith, longing to feel even a twinge of the glow you see in your children?

Giving space for wonder is a choice, and a difficult one for adults. After all, we're the realists, right? We know exactly how long we can stretch an hour and a dollar. We carry the details for each member of our family, keeping track of ALL THE THINGS and ALL THE LISTS. Adulting is hard and also our job, and I daresay we do it well. But no matter how great we are at managing details and tasks, we still need space and time for that which once made our faith childlike.

Bask in the glow that seems to spill from even the dustiest corners of your life. Notice the twinkly lights spreading warmth throughout home and heart. Fully enjoy the delicious foods and treats that come just once a year. Give thanks for the packages and cards arriving in the mail and under the tree. Friend, if you're craving wonder, look no further than the eyes of your own kids, and see the awe in the story of Jesus. On this special day, Christmas Eve, allow wonder to fill your heart and spill over into your every day.

Pray:
Jesus, help me to be humble as a child, and to trust You with childlike faith. Thank you for the way You turn things upside-down in and for Your Kingdom, and thank You for this wondrous day -- the eve of Your birth. Amen.

Ponder:
What deters you from living 'humble as a child'? Is it fear, pride, or something else?

Hands:
Get cozy tonight and make some real-life-wonderful family memories. Surprise each family member with a gift to open - new jammies to wear tonight! Grab everyone's blankets & pillows and snuggle up in front of the Christmas tree. Read the Christmas story from a children's Bible, no matter how old your kids are. It will give an old story new perspective.

December 25:
Christmas Day

At that time the Roman emperor, Augustus, decreed that a census should be taken throughout the Roman Empire. (This was the first census taken when Quirinius was governor of Syria.) All returned to their own ancestral towns to register for this census. And because Joseph was a descendant of King David, he had to go to Bethlehem in Judea, David's ancient home. He traveled there from the village of Nazareth in Galilee. He took with him Mary, his fiancée, who was now obviously pregnant. And while they were there, the time came for her baby to be born. She gave birth to her first child, a son. She wrapped him snugly in strips of cloth and laid him in a manger, because there was no lodging available for them. That night there were shepherds staying in the fields nearby, guarding their flocks of sheep. Suddenly, an angel of the Lord appeared among them, and the radiance of the Lord's glory surrounded them. They were terrified, but the angel reassured them. "Don't be afraid!" he said. "I bring you good news that will bring great joy to all people. The Savior—yes, the Messiah, the Lord—has been born today in Bethlehem, the city of David! And you will recognize him by this sign: You will find a baby wrapped snugly in strips of cloth, lying in a manger." Suddenly, the angel was joined by a vast host of others—the armies of heaven—praising God and saying, "Glory to God in highest heaven, and peace on earth to those with whom God is pleased." When the angels had returned to heaven, the

shepherds said to each other, "Let's go to Bethlehem! Let's see this thing that has happened, which the Lord has told us about." They hurried to the village and found Mary and Joseph. And there was the baby, lying in the manger. After seeing him, the shepherds told everyone what had happened and what the angel had said to them about this child. All who heard the shepherds' story were astonished, but Mary kept all these things in her heart and thought about them often. The shepherds went back to their flocks, glorifying and praising God for all they had heard and seen. It was just as the angel had told them.
Luke 2:1-20

Heart:
You've worked and prepared and now it's here. Merry Christmas, moms! On this joyous and beloved day of days, truly be with your family. Put down the phone, the lists, the expectations, and just be with them. Let go of any ideas you have left of perfection, and embrace your real-life extraordinary. It's all your family really wants for Christmas. It's all He wants for Christmas too.

Pray:
Happy Birthday, Jesus! I am so deeply grateful You came. Today we celebrate You, Lord, Your birth and the life You lived. We love You. Amen.

Hands:
Enjoy this day! Be silly, be love-filled, be present. Wear cheesy matching pajamas and eat too many cookies. Burn the candles down to the wick. Stay up late and go to church. Give thanks, and have a Merry Christmas!

Prayers for Moms at Christmas

These are prayers for you to utter when you've hit a wall, mamas. When thinking of your own words is just too much, when you feel a bit bulldozed by the brevity and swiftness of the season, and when you need a real live Silent Night. When you're in that place, I invite you to pray the prayer you need, and know that I will be thinking of and praying for each of you during this blessed and busy Christmas season.

Much love,
Anna

Prayer for the Parking Lot
Oh Lord. I know you have so, so, SO many more important things to hear and consider. I feel foolish even bringing this to You, yet You said I can talk to You about anything, so here I am. God, first I want to find a parking spot. One that is close to the front door of the store and big enough for my minivan. Then, I'd like my kids to stay near me (instead of running into traffic) as we navigate the parking lot and meander into the store. Finally, when we leave, I'd love to be able to find my car – even if I have to use the panic button on my keychain to make the car honk. Like I said, I know how this sounds. But Lord, I'm asking for grace today. I need some so I

can give some. Thanks, God. Amen.

Prayer for Just One Perfect Place
Lord, if one more kid, or my husband, or even the
cat pokes around underneath the tree again, so help
me I'll toss all the gifts into the garage. I thought it
was pretty good to have everything wrapped
already, and maybe I was asking for it by arranging
them all nicely under the branches. But Lord, I just
wanted one place in the house that looks close to
perfect. I know that's not the goal, but can't I just
have one place? Give me patience, God – I know
my family is just so excited they can't even stand it.
And honestly, I am too. I love Your birthday, Jesus.
Still. Keep the cat out of the tree? Thanks, Lord.
Amen.

Prayer for Family Christmas Dinner
OK. Here we go. We've been cooking and/or
driving all day to get to this dinner. Would you pull
some kind of miracle, God? Help my kids to
remember the manners I've tried so hard to instill.
Could You make sure that they don't declare the
yams "icky," slosh water across the table, or crack
the china? Create space in the hearts of the other
guests for my kids to be kids. Help our extended
family to realize how sweet and dear my kiddos are,
even while they carefully arrange the food on their
plate by color. And will you help me to breathe it all
in deeply, this beautiful mess of our family all
gathered at one table? There are people we miss
dearly who aren't sitting with us this year – may we
allow ourselves to feel that ache, and to be grateful
for the ones who are here in the chairs. We gather in
Your name, Jesus. Amen.

Prayer for Christmas Eve
It's here, Lord -- my favorite night of the whole
year. Not many other nights promise the peace and
joy that this one does, and you know, it almost
always delivers. Sure, I'll be up wrestling with toy
packaging and forgetting to stuff the stockings. And
there's no point in setting the alarm because those
dreaming kids of ours will run in at the crack of
dawn. But as my husband and I will catch each
other's eye across a mountain of discarded plastic
and wrapping paper bits, we'll revel in the wonder
that we get to love our family, and that You
understand every bit of that Love. Thank you for
sending Your Son to be born on this glorious night.
Thank you for beginning His magnificent life with
such an unassuming entrance. His birth sets the tone
for our faith – walk humbly, love mercy, seek
justice. All done in one night in Bethlehem. Grant
me just one moment of quiet peace in front of the
tree tonight? Thank you for coming for me, Jesus. I
adore you. Amen.

Prayer for Christmas Morning
Happy birthday, Jesus! Good grief, it's here
already! That was a very short night. I am so, so
grateful You were born Lord. Would You send me
some extraordinary energy today? Because the kids
who just threw themselves on our bed need me to be
able to keep up with their joy today, and I really
want to. But I need Your help. Thank You for being
joy, and for sending some extra on this day of days.
Now please send coffee and peace. Thank You for
coming, Jesus. We're going to celebrate You big
today.

Prayer for the New Year
There are so many hopes and dreams laid on this
one day, Lord – so many people relying on its
passing to bring a clean slate. And then in two days
when resolutions are already dashed,
disappointment rears. God, You said that You
provide new beginnings each morning as they dawn
fresh with new mercies. Thank you for that. As we
enter a new year, I ask You to stay at the forefront
of our days, that we may claim those new
beginnings and mercies, and that this would be a
blessed year. We know it will be because You are
already there. Thank You, Lord. Amen.

Acknowledgements

This book would not exist without the love and support from a village-full. I'll never be able to adequately thank them for believing in me, in these words, and for physically and literally giving me the time to type them out.

Jared – for so fiercely believing in my words, even and especially when they wouldn't come to mind. You're the gale force to my gentle breeze, the push to my shove, the heartbeat of my life. I'll spend forever trying to tell you how I adore you. Thanks for making me do this.

Sam, Josie and Clara Grace – thank you for watching hours of the Berenstain Bears and Daniel Tiger while Mommy wrote. Thank you for cheering for me – "Go mommy go! You can do it!" I can do it, because of your love. Thank you for making me a mommy. And thank you for being the BEST kids in the whole world. I love you so much!

Mormor – we took over your house by storm and I think you're still picking up the proverbial (and actual) pieces. Thank you for making space for us, and for watching the kids enough for me to crank out a few pages at a time. Thank you for being the safe place to all of your kids. You are so loved.

MOPS at Prince of Peace –Thank you for opening your arms to a new and frazzled and exhausted mom, for welcoming in more of my kids and my mess, for giving us Parent's Mornings Out so I could stare at these pages, and for continuing to provide a place for moms to become themselves bravely, flourishing and starry-eyed.

My (in)courage family – you inspire more than you know. Saul, Lisa-Jo, Mary and Denise – thank you for 'Slacking' with me, for encouraging my quiet dreams to roar, and for following hard after Him. Working and writing alongside you is an honor.

The #realmomconfessions and Girl With Blog communities – you are my people! I am so grateful for you. Thank you for being excited about these moments, for sharing your real life with me and with one another, and for cheering us all on. You all deserve a weekend at the spa and a lifetime supply of chocolate.

And to the One who is Immanuel, who was born into a broken world to break Himself and redeem our hearts… You are the reason for much more than just this season. You are everything. All I have is Yours. Happy Birthday.

About the Author

Anna Rendell is married to Jared, and together they're raising three little kids. Their family (including their golden retriever) lives just outside of Minneapolis, Minnesota. Anna is the Social Media Coordinator and a monthly contributor to DaySpring's incourage.me, and writes real encouragement for real moms at girlwithblog.com. She loves good books, encouraging moms as a speaker and writer, and sipping a peppermint latte by the Christmas tree (which really means grabbing a latte at the drive-thru en route to preschool pickup.)

Connect with Anna online:
Twitter: @anna_r
Facebook: @girlwithblog
Instagram: @girlwithblog
Email: ae.rendell@gmail.com

Share your real mom moments using:
#realmomconfessions
#amomentofchristmas